The Boy from the
War Veterans' Home

POETRY

Faultlines (with Y. Christianse and N. Krouk)
The Great Wall of Instinct
In the Cage of Love's Gradings
Be Straight with Me (for teenagers)
Sensual Horizon
The Human Project: New and Selected Poems
Ground
Eardrum: Poems and Prose about Music

CRITICISM

Microtexts (poetics)
Ngara: Poems, Essays and Meditations (ed. with John Muk Muk Burke)

ANTHOLOGIES

Midday Horizon (ed. with P. Boyle and M. Bradstock)
Harbour City Poems: Sydney in Verse 1788-2008 (ed.)
Contemporary Australian Poetry (ed. with J. Beveridge, J. Johnson and
    D. Musgrave)

APHORISM

Neat Snakes

The Boy from the War Veterans' Home

Martin Langford

PUNCHER & WATTMANN

First published in 2022
Published by Puncher and Wattmann
PO Box 279
Waratah NSW 2298

https://www.puncherandwattmann.com
web@puncherandwattmann.com

ISBN   9781922571250

Cover design and author photo by Tim Langford
Typesetting by Morgan Arnett
Printed by Lightning Source International

 A catalogue record for this work is available from the National Library of Australia

For Syd Langford (1920-1986)

Contents

I

THE BOY FROM THE WAR VETERANS' HOME

(i.m. Syd Langford 1920-1986)

When they pointed you in from the office –
one toothbrush, one hairbrush, one cap –
the men must have wondered: *This is no place for a boy* –
though when phosgene had scraped out their lungs
they had scarcely been more ...

Now they were counting the days as strategic expense.

Whom you must join too.   For TB of the throat.   Doctor said.

So they found you a bed
in a ward for the stoics and shades.

And left you, to lie there, alone.

Did your mum visit? Or write?
What with your brothers, the farm,
and her own hazing mind...

Dad out on Indian railroads...

No doubt the men tried to help.

But eleven is early to find out
the people you need yield to needs of their own.

That the play you are in
may have no scenes where you're not alone.

When a war artist taught you to render,
form was a first, lifelong gift – though with no-one inside it.

A prayer of engagement. Of breathing through line.

While men drowned from blisters and rust.

While the man with no face
walked the man with no limbs in the sun...

While you died more slowly
than anyone else in the ward.

At fifteen they signed you back out –

still unhealed:
since nothing was wrong –
had been wrong from the start –
                  but no longer unhurt.

You watched what the others all did.

You set yourself jaunty, four-square.

But you could not believe you belonged in the room:
that the world had a place
for the boy who could conjure its weight –
who weighed nothing himself.

When *forward* failed,
there was no under-floor to support you –
doubt tumbling loose like a bat-cave of bitterness:
gusts of torn wings at closed doors.

That stayed closed your whole life.

Pat was your great gift:
your anchor – your 'textile Picasso'.

But even great loves don't resolve
into platforms for selves.

And so you sold up and sailed south –
where the light might permit you to re-invent outsets...

where the wound in your luggage
refused to relinquish its right to a mind of its own.

I'm sorry, I'm sorry, you told her.
And she received that as the whole gift it would have been
were it not cruelled by the damage.

What I saw
was pain need not end.

And thus, as I had to, looked *off*.

To get through.

And not to give witness: the curse of the son.

Thank you –
for my sake – and others –
for turning your rage on yourself –
for the rough human sums.

Nature, they say, abhors vacuums.

But nothing Mum did
could have given this nihil a floor:

lost, at your easel,
for somewhere to start –
for motion to enter your hand –
to make up for there being nothing
you needed to draw ...

Nothing, you'd rasped, *to be said*.

– Something to test, with my life.

If I gave grief,
I was trying for upright.

Then only helplessness:

watching you twitch
from the trenches, redoubts, you had dug –
as the Huntington's bit –
the unselving disease –
that no-one, this time, had picked up.

II

THE PRAYER TO STORY

Save me, O Story,
from unstructured moments –
rooms without histories,
streetscapes without conversations.

Fill up my dead time with sequence:
I don't require substance or style –
uncluttered rhythms,
the ironic eyebrows of art –
as long as the tales are strong-boned –
as long as there's room for a guest
to feel warm in a role.

Supply my encounters with plots.

Let the fall of the cards
become plausible arrows of time.

Strike out the great void
and push on through stutter or pause
before silence sneaks in.

Above all, O Narrative,
guide me across
untranslatable others:
teach me the slurs
to glide over their presence,
the syntax
that keeps them in place.

Guard me
from the clarities of textures,
the vertigo of naked skin,
the wastes of light.

Type layers of Garamond,
veils of Calibri,
over the sci-fi of green life,
the terrors of red.

Lose me in your tentacles,
enlarge me with your swells.

Enslave me with doubt,
and direct my each step towards closure –

Settle, O Story, my fears,
and re-institute peace,
with the witchery-drums of arrival.

MIDGES

A neurasthenic trampoline of midges –
in a late patch of sun after rain:

not too much time now
to make sure their stories come right.

THE MASTER OF TALES

The *quillipy-lip-lip-quorrop* of the swift parrot
stutters and fades in the eucalypt's crown,
so it will not be seen
by the story of handsome-sized paddocks
with unbroken views.
The rat-kangaroo hurls through grass
like a rocket on wheels – until it expires, saucer-eyed –
fleeing the lovable saga of Mumbles the Cat.
Light-bombed, quolls scurry and sniff for a limb –
away from the tale of the waterfront auctions –
though gnarly, worn rock can do nothing –
but wait – and pray dozers are quick –
when epics of Scale start to rumble –
those hard-angled, office-block giants,
their exultant plans...

Even however, if, one day,
the soft noise of stories dismembers the earth –
so nothing is left but a dry scrape at dusk,
a powder of animal bones –
it won't affect me, because *I* am the Master of Tales.
I will dive like a start-up through deep inconvenience –
surface, hours later, with tips about how to move on.
No drought will temper my courage;
no fire dismay me, no burnt shade of ego's mistakes –
croaking for water and laid low by heat,
I will still be too smart, too significant:
in my world, where stories renew –
where heroes can never *be* scripted
as other than charming – resourceful – unharmed.

KNITTING

At the Royal North Shore,
the builders' first task
was to hang up a two-storey canvas –
a pencil-and-wash
of the old nurses' quarters –
so nobody's eyes were offended
by screes of grey waste.

Shop-fitters board up their windows
to guard us from fit-outs.

Show compères burble through pauses
so silence won't win...

And the job of the adult's
to knit up a matrix of stories –

to knit and to knit:

to discover, unpick and stitch up
every flaw, every gap:

knit until Christmas, and then some;
knit until Dr Oncology points to your seat;
knit and purl one till the human design
reaches all the way up to the mountain;
knit till it floats on the water;
knit till it suffocates
every unpasteurised germ...

knit like you're only one half-stitch away
from a rent in the fabric so wide
you can't help but fall through.

THE CAPITALIST'S TALE

You walk out in landscapes
where nothing exists
but your needs:
barbed wire –
to guard your possessions,
cameras –
for those whom you love.

No textures –

no living thing
with a life of its own.

You work on your story,
but have no idea what the point is.

You cannot imagine past triumph
to what might come next.

Announce a new start:
all you get
is more windowless signage –
more figures slumped
into terms of convenience –
pre-emptive headings
by which they are yarded
so far past the kindness you'd dreamt of –
the warmth you might share...

What are these tally marks, traveller?

What is the name of the wide air
you're pegging out now?

BENEATH US

This, too, is what we have built –
layer on layer of rank-sodden grief –
debris from Self-Esteem House:
down where the choices
haunt St James's tunnels,
the Tank Stream distributes its tears:
down with the stares of indifference,
blank looks in which others drown...
This is where the true love of the fifties ended up –
in re-appraisals, post-ejaculation;
here, too, the replays of finicky smiles,
the sighs on the wrong side of yes:
a parallel city of distance, rejection –
the logic of *either* and *or* ...
as soon as we learnt to make judgements:
to push our way through as brave, self-writing heroes –
scattering unwanted stories, declaring our aims –
smiling, loquacious but blunt – kissing this, dissing that...

III

HEAD OF VESPASIAN

Confident, shrewd and dependable:

the Romans built a world
out of features like these –

and their closed, self-referential self-imagining:
moles of an interior progression
through the opiates of rank.

Respect, then, of a kind, where it is due:
to Vespasian, and all his stolid processes –
to all those who have managed in his stead –
plotting the shopping-paths,
raising the hill,
designing the labels and brands
for the plague-human eye...

The freezer shelves are full, as one would wish.

The borders are secure; the workers calm.

But who is going to lead me to the other?

AIRPORT

At the airport, there is flat space
and burnt space; bright space, and space
dull with cloud. It is plotted with lines,
so the travellers can tell where they stand.
Nose up, the great ships descend out of thinness
and falter their way through the colours. Soon,
they will nudge the peninsulas, beasts at a crib:
wait – in a trance of vast shadows –
while lovers embrace in a meadow of luggage,
guests of the lines drawn on sky.
This is the peace of the body – arrival,
          and proof.
                    They do not have long,
but hold tight, while the red numbers flail,
to the cliff-face of brief, warm exemption –
who know what time is –
and how, soon, they must leave
for the realms where the word-monsters reign –
for the games of what others are thinking –
of managing story,
of working out what words want next.

ANTIQUE SHOP

The shop's
        at the visible end
of the infinite well:
   where wintry light's met
   by a few tattered lamps –
edging and shading
the faces of those in its aisles –

        who,
        also subdued,
do not plough through treasures –
   but turn them, and tilt,
and invite the scuffed flotsam to speak...

        émigré postcards –
   amnesiac dresses and rings –
        lockets,
        requests for relief –

           each object
stained by the hazards of absence:
   tarnished disjecta
from homelessness/ intimate warmth –
        dust in the attic
   or prayers at the debutantes' ball –

        beyond which
   lie echoless caverns...

Untethered,
      glinting spill waits
for reprieve from the gloom:

      splinters of eros
adrift on the disheveled skin
            of what does not exist.

AIR DANCERS

The frayed dudes with ecstatic dreads
are too happy for words.
They are happy because air is pumped –
at industrial speeds – up their raggedy bums.
They are happy because they're unique:
with moves of their own at the elbow and wrist,
and old-fashioned, cutely pursed lips...
They jiggle and waggle and never lose courage –
but shimmy and twist when it's raining –
boogie when nobody's there.
They are happy because with these margins
the staff will make *quids*.
Because sales are *so* good at deals!
They're so stoked they love the aesthetics:
caryards at twilight – with Venus and moon;
the beckon and gleam of new models
in low showroom light...
And concrete: they *love* all that concrete.
Cambers! And vanishing points!
They're happy because they are tactics:
old hands with deftly-worked branding –
and flags that wave too!
Because, in the shots of the yard,
they are *there* – in the forecourt!
And because they're surrounded by road noise:
when – guess what? *Their job's to sell cars!*
        They know there are deaths
and bad smells and infectious diseases.
But also how vital good attitude is.
Right from the moment they'd first been installed,

they would stand to attention, and quiver –
let cold air fart from the tops of their heads,
and then spasm and flail and collapse –
just to shudder up straight, straight away –
because theirs is the best workers' mindset –
to do what you must, to the max, and then do it again.

THE GOOD WORKER

In Xinjiang, the clear-eyed and noble
are nursing a land. People like you:
who are loyal and keen –
who can't do enough to repay
the kind words of the strong.
It is no little thing
to re-schedule a whole people's thinking.
You must re-write their old lives,
and re-build their mosques as plain air.
You must prove that their previous joys
were just smears of bad film.
These are not commonplace talents.
It takes wit and patience
to calibrate cameras, write stout curricula,
order the neatest barbed wire.
You sit through dull meetings, write memos;
make stolid journeys
to regions which need your firm hand.
Then: when the team leader
singles you out for your focus –
your shrewdness, esprit – you juice up inside
in that sac where euphoria foams.
You watch the kids play in your side-street:
their smiles dispense power to your stride.
You watch your wife sleeping,
but make no connection
with others who wait, late at night,
for the sharp crunch of gravel,
the sick, swinging lights. Bearer
of seamless accords between language

and hormone, and hormone and role,
no questions cloud your contingencies.
It may be you'll never be conscious:
your clear-sighted gaze always
vigilant, earnest and blind.
But, when you float out of being –
your task still unfinished
though so many broken and bowed –
it's hard not to think
you won't hover and glow, with content,
at the difference you've made:
a fast-stiffening corpse of achievement –
a strawberry rictus
of pleasure and rigour and pride.

THE AMBITIONS

When I think of the lives of the elbow –
of, *I want that job*,
and,
Who gives a rat's arse
who gets hurt? –

what I see
is slow rain on the ocean:
random and unnumbered endings –
crater first – pimple – then rings –
a grey calm at twilight;
horizonless, sibilant hush.

1.02° RISE: MIDSUMMER, CHATSWOOD

A day which vanishes
down every street.

All signposts point to pale vistas.

Gleaming roofs oscillate,
six inches out from their walls.

Plane trees are fizzing miasmas.

Bodies jive blurred poly-rhythms
contracting downhill.

Clouds glide like lives
out through contexts.

And even though all of the houses
are schmicked-up just so:

tidiness makes no impression –

this heat is playing with absence
and serious things.

THREE CITIES

In Vegas: the child's dream of power without cost.
In LA: the dream of the young man – of power at whatever the cost.
In Frisco: the daydream of adults –
of what might lie out there, beyond power – and whether it's real.

GAMES

Sick, sick of the games.

Release-of-information games
to maximise the pleasures of crime-fiction.

Auteur's identity-cues –
so the audience knows
whose anxieties *it* needs resolved.

CV e-labyrinths.

Pub-chaff charades.

Exchanges of stories in bed...

As if when love flares, it says,
'Fools, let the contest begin...'

Is this how it's been
since we first took our oaths in the court
and stood up to air spin?

Solitudes tuned
to the old dream of loving so closely
you'd know who this was?

Lovers who've argued
and turned to the wall, and turned back:

who know too that everything changes –

the tales they've just heard,
and the tales they themselves have made up –
guesses and wounds on the pale, bruised arena
of *How much?* and *Always?* and *When?*

This is not the only place
where people lay their heads against the word
and weep and pray –
but this is where the distance feels like home:

again   and again   and again

till language folds over   and buries itself in the sand.

THE DISAPPEARED

Super 8, Kodachrome, digital –
year after year, there are children who wave
from the pool while the dog barks along.
Cypresses. Foam on the car.
        Smiles turn to tears –
and then Mother appears with the drinks...

Next scene: the sun is still shining –
cloudless skies flicker away –
but there's someone not there:
the three friends who posed at the football,
the posse of kids who had fought for the bat
all day long: they have all grown so big!

        Except one:
who has left to be somebody else.

Who had thought there were –
        somewhere –
more potent, more credible days.

Who had packed in a hurry,
and left without scribbling a note –

        but who'd thought
there would always be someone...

Who had had no idea that the street
was so huge, so available.
That the life of the free might mean

counting the hours, for the man.
That after the first john,
there's no phoning home. That heists
write their own plots and gags...

Waking in single-room flats,
with their skies of pearl-grey – to the ticking
of deadlines. Finding your best friend
asleep by your side, but not breathing.
Stealing from parents and howling in clinics:
the beautiful faces, the hard-cores,
the well-spoken boys –

Were the episodes worth it?

Did the verismos of Narcan and ambulance
panic with more authenticity –
weep with more truth –
than days of impatience with cupcakes,
banter in which there was no room
for uncensored futures, unrealised claims?

THE HOSTESS OF SMILES

Soon, there'll be nothing but pretty
wherever I go –
smiles to entice me inside,
to invite me to smile.
The pretties don't smile for themselves,
but for needs that have paid them.
Still, it is nice to pretend they are pretty
for me. Soon – by extension –
the scrub will be pavement,
and vacant lots – units and shops.
The unkempt, ambiguous earth
will be concrete and lawn.
Our lives will be spent
on the orderly skins
of design-teams. No mess
from still-to-matures,
or the shortly-decrepit:
the first signs of smudge,
and the Neat Squad will make
their erasures. Signs of disorder
persisting, The Hostess of Smiles
will lean out from her hoarding:
her great lips tilt forward –
huge cliffs of immaculate red –
her smile lift and freeze – just enough –
so there can be no misunderstanding.

STROP

When Stroppa stepped out of the pub
into optimum day, he was walking okay –
all the steadier still
once his flourish and bow stopped the cars –
and bigmouths and horns
felt obliged to have something to say.
Strop was a good bloke –
so he started singing – *con brio* –
Be happy, and walked even slower –
and stopped, when he came to the woman
whose car had beeped first:
to sing – with an all-day-wide smile –
Don't worry, be happy,
and bang on her bonnet,
and go on his way with a wave.
Airborne, and stronger inside: stronger than lawyers
or exes; than kids screwing up.
Stronger than sleeping in bus-stops; than jumped-up
and ad hoc farragoes they'd shoved in his face
for the whole of his life – business, politeness;
the rivers that flow to the Murray;
the value of patience; the slick and coercion of dates.
This was more like it:
the green of a damp, shining streetscape;
the torsos of gum-trees; the long queue of cars at his back.
This was the place to be: inside his happiness.
Why had it taken so long to have figured things out?

THE GUIDE

We'd thought we were free to look round.

But she led us to where all the visits begin,
and then waited...
                    to speak without pause –
with deft modulations at each new exhibit:
        wobbling her head,
with a smile, so our gazes don't stray.

We are quizzed to make sure we've been listening –
fed favourite details to nestle us
under her wing...

                The old house is pretext.

As long, she believes, as she keeps
overwhelming the punters with perfect technique –
she won't have to enter a space someone else might be in.

ETTALONG

Saturday morning, and everything's
cheerful and new.
Robbo is washing the Holden.
Desley waves steaks in both hands.
Even where yards are neglected,
sunbeams are streaming, paspalum nods,
hedges are glistening with dew. Chook's
Sopwith windvane whirrs slowly.
Old Yarborough's fence is a stave –
with the notes to a song.
Drinkers lean back on pub benches.
Shadows lean wide on pub steps.
Small, out on flats by the channel,
big dogs, like elegant cut-outs,
tumble and leap
against frozen, silk reaches of blue.

EXCITED

A railway track.
A giant ute.
Toys that respond when you speak.
That light up when they're touched.

Envoys of love from his folks –
that seek love in return:

though he cannot quite give them
the cues that they want –

he is young, and distracted by toys...

What can they do
except lean in and point –

their voices a cautious ensemble
of slightly tense notes?

THE SCRATCHINGS

In a room with an outlook –
a forest of warm, subtle uprights –
of luminous line –
an old man is listening intently,
his eyes on the ground:

because the murmur
of the scratchings, and the form,
can lead him through the afternoons
more gently than the colours of the sun.

CREMATORIUM

Neither practised ad-lib
from the man with the pointy cream slip-ons,
nor the bugless composure of roses,
can quite keep our gaze
from the bloom and esprit of the smoke.

GAME THEORY: THE SUIT

Sometimes your choices weren't choices:
for the sake of the game – of game-theory –
let's say that they were.
Let's call it a choice – a mistake –
to be born in a family
that wasn't concerned
if you made it to school.
A choice not to learn how to read.
A choice – a mistake – to succumb
to the way power dealt tricks
in your playground and streets.
A mistake not to plan for the future.
A mistake to be ugly.
To think that a life on the dole
was as good as it gets.
A mistake to get married.
And then for your wife to walk out
after twenty-three months.
A mistake to have done what you did.
So many mistakes till the one mistake left
was to wear this improbable suit –
with your hair plastered down on your bald patch,
and your air of respect, and defeat –
to have thought for one moment the judge
might examine the jacket –
and riffle, once more, through his notes:

to sit there, and blush, and look down,
in your special exhibit: to pluck at its sleeve
with the mildest of all legal arguments;

to proffer its loose, crumpled plea
against all you're accused of –
its scuffed, shapeless flare of resistance
to what happens next.

TO BE KNOWN

Only a lover
can heal
the desire to be known.

Though only a lover
will wonder, all night,
just who it is
lying beside them.

THE DOOR FASCISTS

We can tell at a glance:

we're the line
between promise and failure –
the gulf between brands.

Sometimes, yes,
we are inscrutable.

Mostly our choices
need no explanation:

who only enact
what you also believe:
that some must be left in the street.

How, without judgement
can beauty be given a value?

How – without hard calls like ours –
would you know whom to love?

SINGING

While Mum's in the shop
and the tourists stroll by,
seagulls tilt shoulders
and Neilla and Bon,
in the backseat,
start singing a song:
a tune like the mild, sunny morning –
not showy, no big notes –
an unstudied chorus
of listening and working as one –
of treble, intent distillation –
not waiting for signals,
not drifting from pitch –
but pleased to know all of the lyrics –
and pleasure in hearing them sung...
till Mum gets back in
and they strain
to see what she has bought them –
the talk heads elsewhere
and the song is forgotten:
off into unfocused waves
and entropic dispersals –
at one with the earth's coldest nights.

AMERICA

Their land was so rich.

Why wouldn't God seem
like the shape that one wished to become?

I'm not saying we are less selfish.

But Australia's been sparser, and drier:
selves can seem more like conditions
one learns to accept.

Not: *freedom to swallow one's others,*
one's dream is so righteous;

but: *freedom –*
because there is no other choice –
to settle on joint understandings –
with room for one's own.

SHORTS

SAFE PASSAGE

Vatic, parsimonious, surprising:
his style – like an uptilted chin –
glided through salons
unhampered by meaning's sharp edges.

BARE

Low tide and white horses:
salt wind has stripped my mind bare,
and my words are just froth…

RELEASE

Both the otherness of the forest
and the otherness of the crowd
release me –
if just for a short time –
from terms of exchange.

COMMONS

Slow rain –
and everything mild and exact:
a commons of light without shadows.

THE MANNEQUIN'S LEG

The mannequin's leg
angles out from her hips –
as if towards beauty –
as if it were some other place.

THE LAST BIRD

Even the last bird
will throw back its forehead
and chirrup and twitter and tweet
in the way that birds do.

LIVE TRADE

Each night I keep waking up:
how will my loved ones survive
if we can't mistreat animals?

KANIMBLA VALLEY

Angles, intensities, mist:
light slants and drifts
like a pageant of national claims.

ON A REVIEW OF A GARDENING BOOK
BY THE POET, MARK TREDINNICK

'The problem is, I don't like gardens...'

But Mark, poems also
are spaces
where the construct
and autochthon co-exist...

UNTITLED

What does one have,
come the end,
but the frail arm of beauty?

LILITH

When they built a second storey
on the corner –
it's a real estate now –
between Station, and Peat's Ferry Road
(this would have been in the twenties) –
their new leadlight windows
were abstract-nouveau understatements
that make me think *Lilith* –
the lilac-and-pastel, perhaps,
they would use for such things.
This was no Hornsby of bluchers
and billiards. They wore suits to work,
and wrote letters to Councillor Smythe.
They were building an empire
of practical selfishness: double-brick
bungalows snaked along ridges
that led on to ridges
the new houses snake along now.
The Charleston. The Cha-Cha.
The Quickstep. With one-twos
to Elvis, and Prince. While dresses
swished by, and the draughtsmen
sketched blunt marginalia.

       It may be the whole plateau,
soon, will be dark, beneath walls –
whose owners nurse dreams
of an intimate cruelty,
dressed up as *Home and Away*:
whose daydreams trail off
into tableaux of unowned contempt...

who ground their beliefs
in a bed's paranoia
and practise good manners at work;
whose stories declare that to love,
and to own, are distinct...
       Who still walk to work
where those pale understatements
stare blankly at littorals of light.

THE WOUND

I can't remember
when I last read a love poem
from a man to a woman.
There are poems of affection
after long years together,
poems of grief
for things that didn't happen,
things that did.
But if a man
praises a woman,
the mike switches on,
the cameras light up,
and someone pounds up
to inquire
who he thinks that he is.

The men understand
there will have to be change.

What to do?

While the women retire?

Who do not know either –
who pace,
with stern looks, but few plans –

neither acknowledging
  justice
may only be possible

if love and status
aren't joined at the hip:

a wound for the ages –

though not –
a few gestures aside –
under current review.

KNOWLEDGE

(Something in us II)

Something in us
needs to know.

It is our fate to be questions –

to make up proposals
whose answers
come laden with distance –

to utter ourselves
farther off
with the trompe l'oeil of words:

who cannot return –
save in poems;

or move on –
save by knowing more stuff:

ghosts
of the sign's smooth displacements –

its wonders, its cures.

GUIGNOL

Firing squads...

pits where free thinkers must jump to conclusions...

the number-aesthetics involved in displaying the skulls...

When I was younger,
I hunted the wastes of guignol.

I wanted to know what the worst was:
to set my beliefs on firm ground.

Now, I'm light-phobic:

if there's a book on Rwanda,
a report on the camps in Xinjiang –
I will set it aside.

It's not just that outrages sit and won't shift –
like bad lines in a poem...

I'd thought they were *other* –

that I was immune.

Now I see *I* am disease.

With no other choice
but to frequent considerate rooms –

to keep it at bay
with the shrewdest, most kind-hearted talk –
the nimblest regrets and demurs.

WEIGHTLESS

The surfaces are clean, and nothing sticks.

Every joke is certified cost-free.

Windows and silences –
even depth here's
just a pinball of cultural reflections.

Click off your date, there's no sighing.

Click off the birds, and who cares?

They never were
more than glimpses and aerodynamics...

As long as you're free.

A spider that rides the wind's currents.

Weightless and gliding
through so many preferences
none of them count for a thing:

a tone that's not sharp, and not flustered;

a banter of easy recall
without stumble or doubt...

though alert
to the weight of the moment –

to readings so subtle – or strange –
they loosen – if just for a moment –
the planet-wide project to make all experience
equable, distant and kind.

WINNERS

Number is their true Penelope:
what use are figures of speech
if the things *they* play tag with
are vagrant as sighs?

Numbers allow proper precedence.

Numbers allow one to figure out
just where one stands –

not like those wastelands
where nobody wins –
which feel like you've been left alone
in the very last room – and with no idea why.

The most potent garlic's reserved
for encounters with others:
lovers or galaxies, country or poems:
what can one *do* with such sphinxes?

What bribe or spell
could reduce *them* to scores in your shade?

Holidays,
winners get restless by lunchtime –
fidget for rivals...
            get antsy for contests, or proofs.

Aimless –
till threats reappear:

till the need to prevail restores calm –

winning will keep them on track
with its steep dreams of loss...

Then, when death nears,
there's a mattress
of claims and achievements:
winners die plausibly –
and with a healthier brisket –
write neater endings,
and always have shinier teeth –

sliding away from the light –

while earnest comparatives
flutter from stories and tears
to the eulogist's feet:
a thin mulch of last relativities,
a swirl of hierarchical bows –

till new numbers, firming elsewhere,
stir through the adjectives –
raise a congenial murmur –
new hope for rank and degree.

THE CAMPS

I lived, for a while,
in the weatherboard barracks at Bradfield.
It was where I learnt swearing,
and how to be too tough for ties –

though I still needed shoes:
the airmen before us
had littered the camp with hilarities.
Like the troops, we were just passing through.

The place was a slum, but a chrysalis-slum:
a halt between future and past,
where you practised transitions.
Sydney Cove, Bendigo, Tumut:

what sites more characteristic –
what mood more Australian? –
rule-hazy, goal-hazy clearings
that shrugged off the past,

but provided few prompts;
where newcomers stared –
without guidelines – at brilliance and scrub,
as the unmoored still do – now all homes

are campsites, all contexts ad hoc,
in the bitter-sweet scrum of the sign.

ARRIVAL

They had trekked –
from the time before records –
away from the sword, and its henchmen;
the prince's one tale, and its rules.
For the error of not being tribal,
they'd been wheeled into live shows and eaten.
For the crime of preferring their freedom –
   nailed high to crosses,
each milestone from Rome to the sea.
They had trekked for the right to believe,
and the right to refuse to:
threading escape-lines, and borders –
sweating down paths
that led straight towards roll-calls in gulags –
jokes at which nobody laughed
in tired, windowless rooms.

But their colleagues ploughed on:

rolling the phonemes of justice
around on their palates;
warming the faint, outlaw hope
they might be whom they chose –

retching on 'tween decks,
and sharing out water in dinghies;
bribing the guards
to recalculate visas and dates...

Only to find
that arrival
is where things begin.

That the next suite –
though real –
is conceptual:

but that nobody weeps
for the lack
of what fear cannot see.

That the motifs they'd steered by
could take such an easy back-seat
to the courtyard, the talk –
where gestures are tensioned
by mobile, erotic inflections –
effortless readings of status –
the way stories firm, in the sun...
while pigeons peck on, for their living,
and the street is a scarf of bright offers –
scrolling through answers
they'd once tried to leave far behind –
trailed round their necks
like the noose it could happily be.

THE LAUGH

They won't tear up all of the books:
just those that trace the subversions
of meaning and touch –

                       insist
on the existence of the other...

Romance and Adventure will remain –
the dazzled-by-power
will still reach for the drugs of esteem.

Auntie will go –
if there's anything left –
though news-shows by then
may too rarely be worth the deleting:
together, however,
they'll reference a dissident mood.

That frail, sunlit moment
in which, in a few places,
people could think for themselves,
will revert into myth:
only the brave will suggest
that such things may have been.

The cameras have all been installed,
and their pupils are live.

Every slight move
will be cross-/double-checked
for the files.

Many will die,
so the hormone of triumph rests easy.

Fear will sit deep in our eyes,
and its lies will ring true –
the Corps of Anonymous Endings
call by, anytime.

But even if no-one can move,
for the next hundred years –
  nor think,
because all thoughts are miked;
even if rivers of blood
we'd so wanted to dam,
just start flowing again –

the dancing
will not be extinguished:

someone

will drop a poem into a silence

logic will flower
to an unblinking gaze

somehow

somehow   somewhere

the screaming will flex
to the laugh
of a mischievous child.

IV

THE MOONCALVES

Most art's just power for the senses:
wafers of ego –
make-up with lights – and slick skills.
Not wonder or dance – calculation:
spells for one's narrative –
trading-rights, party-tricks, bluff.
Court after self-impressed court –
by which we might understand one thing –
the power of the prince. Carpets and ivory –
measured in eyesight. Hall after hall
of the portraits of those who could pay.
Old tricks and cunning perspectives:
of making the hero look nobler, look taller;
of leading the eyes up the stairs,
to The Site of His Highness's Prick.

Of scoring the trumpets and choir
so you, too, praise Culloden...

Lenses for prestige,
and scripts for the hormones of dreamers,
the glands of the tribe...

      With knight-moves
for modern enhancements:
fashion, expression *and* taste;
downloadable democracies
where everyone can dream of kissing rank.
Flowers for the starlet, and wreaths of young men
for the star: a foyer of photo-shopped
prospects, *at ease* with their abs.

Art for complacencies.

Art for the engorgement of the pitch...

Sometimes it seems
that the mooncalves with big, mournful eyes –
the slow ones who mumble past status –
are all that we have...

Schubert. Or Issa. Giorgione.

All their works pointless – or less –
if they can't be parlayed
into networks or views:

Tu Fu is calming
his unfurnished exile to brushstrokes.

Nadehzda and Osip
have just received news they must go.
They walk, one last time, in the forest.
The cliff that has hunted them,
night after night, in their dreams,
is devouring the sky...

They don't buy much glamour,
these ink trails –
disconsolate spoors
for the textures of time and its wounds –

that neither save others,
nor those they are made by:

but offer, at least, a relief
from the howls of advantage –
wheeling down cycles of sunset –
the swarms of the triumphs:
exultant, but joyless, and thin.

ART, LOVE AND WAR

There is a Stella Bowen painting from the thirties:
Art, Love and War. Two couples talk
in a Provençal garden with eager, but uncertain gazes.
About whether Germans would really be worse
than their own lot; workers would ever be free...
What truth was: leaders – and art-forms.
It could have been my parents – *art and injustice.*
On their planet, all would be welcome –
except for the cruel. They spoke for the virtues
of working-class skills, modernist painting,
fair play. This was the humanist moment: the good
would prevail. When Dad sketched nudes,
it was homage: nor did Mum ask of her fishermen
anything awkward – like *bycatch* or *cod.*
As if art were versions of mercy: maquettes
of warm intent; kind, pencilled slabs of white stone.
In one shot, my mother leans back on a draft
of a mural – a child of her moment, with gifts.
My father looks up from his workbench –
evasive, bemused. While all the self-interests
scrape furtively, out past the doorway. How shall I manage
their subtle and Protean antics? What could I do but refuse?

LEATHER ELBOWS

They worked as volunteers in the Reading Room.
They were part-time stewards for the Union.
Read R.H.Trelawney, synopses of Plato;
tried Esperanto, *Co-operative Practices: Accounts*.
Not drinkers, they could become stubborn
at lunch over Christmas. Few of them
fought for the mana of hold-the-floor humour –
their decencies baulked. But they did become hot
at advantage. So they signed up
for struggles whose terms were evasive –
whose tales of injustice were clear: affronted
by wrongs others turned a blind eye to;
dreaming of thank-you's from workers
who dreamt other things. Most of them fought,
although most thought that wars were for business.
A few got to Uni. A few produced jazz shows,
wrote background for ABC news.
Most were worn down by the dutiful, dry repetitions.
The privileged laughed. And the worker might too.
Neither believed that mere words could interrogate status.
But outrage – and habit – still drove them –
till bright waves of shtick
left them nowhere to picket – or dream.
Much that they fought for will crumble
if all gestures fold to bouquets of self-interest.
But I thank them, all the same, for having thought of me.
Nowadays, in Australia, even poems are largely written
in the spaces that they won: clearings that spilled out
and multiplied – so unexpectedly – messily, wide.

THE BRISBANE LONGEURS

They didn't talk to each other, of course.
They talked to themselves.
Later they would say things to the page.
But – Peter and Kevin, David and Rhyll –
they all of them got them –
those inward looks vacant as sky.
They were part of their childhood –
like tears – or the way that words lie:
like heat which slowed air to a shuffle;
composts of leaf-shadow abstracts
downhill from the gate; wirelesses
broadcasting seed-grain
in ABC-formal; fences
dividing the hills like the march of alone...
Peter trawled toes over gravel;
David's nose pressed against glass –
thought-bubbles mooning for action...
which set out for places
where ideas came layered in deeds –
where beauty was more than a cold one;
in which the un-netted took shape:
in which they could spiral
with signature bourrées and leaps –
twirl with adjustments in tone –
coruscate, twitter
in salons where lost afternoons
had everted to friendships and work:
a dance-list with real steps and monsters –
suites of deft gestures with which to disarm
the unmannerly questions of suits...

Till – as is the way
with the word's disregard for the clock –
sooner than anyone knew,
it was time to diffuse; as promptly
as egress had foamed in the first place,
all that was left
were the caves of sky blue
that had dreamt them all those years ago –
a vanishing ballast of objects,
a moist breeze of favourite lines –
still urgent, and still inexplicable –
but milder now, poignant –
like everything vivid
discoloured by stains of farewell.

PETER PORTER

When he decided, in the fifties,
that poetry was not yet possible in Australia –
sailing away on the SS Inquiry Observer –
did he understand that once
he had been whispered by tradition,
nothing in its terms
would let his origin be visible again?

Except as Eden –
pointlessly attractive, and impervious to words.

And spiking every text he sailed towards.

THE PROSE POEM

He had known, straightaway, it was a prose-poem, by its modest tone and its elegance. Besides, the lighting was subdued – a dusk in which the browns were almost black. Gradually – 'at the civilised pace that the prose poem adopts' – he saw others there too. The girl he had loved in his twenties slid through: prompting not grief, but dismay, at their unaligned views. Next, came a column of rotund authorities, all travelling backwards, and each on a tilt; each one extruding a bright little tuft of pronouncement – maxims drifting away into flocculent air. Then he entered a robust discussion. It must have been lively, judging by the impression of wit it exuded, but he had no idea what it was about. The discussion reappeared as a pair of string sculptures passing threads through each other's arms – though both participants seemed aware that this could never be as satisfying as an exchange of actual views. The sculptures vanished; the floatees grew thinner, and faded; he began to encounter dead-ends: a tunnel that only went part of the way through the hill; a rail-line that stopped at a buffer; a loading bay without a shop. The metaphors were so clunky, he became self-conscious: the text was in danger of collapsing. It would have ended then and there, had he not blacked out, and forgotten where he was: a little charade of uncertainty by the prose-poem, an awkward moment of fourth-wall anxiety for the protagonist, and the whole thing resumed, and he was on his way...

Which was better than unconsciousness, but not to the extent that it led anywhere. He put his notebook in his pocket. There did not seem much point in recording things which were incapable of interaction, even if they were mildly interesting. He knew, when he stepped outside again, he would still be on his own. The prose-poem just made it more obvious – a cell of stylish passivity, where agency had neither been proposed nor encountered. No matter, it seemed, how attentive he was, nor with how much tact he attempted to interact, his companions would still just glide past, each in its non-negotiable world. Even when he found himself in an embrace – but who was this? – by the time he had adjusted his weight, and aligned for the kiss, the prose-poem had taken him by the hand, and led him, protesting and confused, out, through his companion, to the street – where a Scottie dog was barking at his shoes. Back, it seemed, to all the comic turmoil of necessity.

CHARMIAN

Charmian,
it wasn't your fault:
the great shifts had already stirred –
you were game for their news.
As soon as you saw that the Father and Male
would no longer be cupped by the God –
as soon
as there was nothing but our words –
all your choices had been made.
Because you had the confidence of beauty;
because your Dad had taught you
to be scared of being scared:
you stood on the star-lip of every dilemma and dived –
    to find trust was a curse:
that no-one could stomach the meanings of words –
nor answer the prayer of your touch.
As George could not stomach your men –
though he might understand.
As you could not face them yourself,
in your small-township nights.

When he took his revenge like an author –
writing you into his novel and out of your life –
he still couldn't handle the trope you'd become:

a diving Miranda –
an impulse abstracted to light –

    who steadies herself for release...

You will fuck up –
because, being jealous,
we'll make sure you do –

and because you are human yourself.

But just at this moment,
you're one with the sea and the stars.

Now, as you take that deep breath,
and rise up on your toes...

THE SUICIDES

(Berryman, Jarrell, Sexton et al)

It was their honesty that killed them –
that stealth machine –
who had all read their Yeats, played with stilts;
knew how a metaphor stiffened a backbone –
were proud, and forensic, and prickly...

Who laughed in love's face, as they re-wrote its hymns;
scorned reputation, but wrestled and wept on its rungs:

who found themselves naked, with only their egos –
and nothing to keep the tent up, but the noise of the show...

If the god had fallen sideways from their poems,
they would have to explain who they were –
why they juggled such claims –

nights of re-routing the smashed roads to grandeur;
of nursing incurable themes –
of daring their jokes down the hill towards absolute noir:
waking to empties,
and rivals who'd witnessed their nightmares,
their underscored proofs...

What can one do
with the Laurels of Flensed Exaltation –
but burn them
by saying what happened?

AVANT-GARDE

A vast line of trump cards with dildoes –
each one buggering the next –

faster and faster as progress progresses:

until the last one disappears
up its very own bum.

The Trump of All Trumps!

The Great Artwork!

Like a last, irrevocable *Fuck You!*
to dreams of *Me Next!*

THE CHORUS

Whether in Handel –
He Shall Reign Forever –

or Red Army basses,
asserting their pax
across rumours of Gulags/fake news:

choruses denoted
the submission
of the individual will.

Now, when the space
around utterance is fragile –
unstable –
      though open:
so subjects can breathe –

shall we ever again
sing as one?

THEORY

Theory will manage
your terror
of meeting the artwork –

with rulings
for every new flourish –

a slash of discernment
for every encounter:
colleague, anthology, panel –
your partner, your clothes...

Nestled – entrenched –
in its battlements,
this earth can feel
like a place
even you might belong –

though all dwellings shift –

and one thing that theory
can't banish
is doubt about theory...

THE HAGFISH

The hagfish have wriggled inside.

They nuzzle and suck at my neck-bones,
mucous past elbow and knee...

As soon as they've finished,
I'll sail on – a pale sack of vellum
distending its arms –
a slow-motion rage of neat words –

torn tubes of verse
reaching out with their fingers and toes...

A flag of still-live possibilities –
plausible phrases,
conjectures and bon mots and tropes...

As soon as the fat ones
have slid
through the holes in my skull:

I'll take to the sea-lanes –
a pennon of dermis,
unwavering banner of will –
soggy, but forthright, in deep-ocean style –
out beyond critics, and prizes,
out beyond details like death,
and the absence of light...

GOYA'S DOG

When Goya's dog
got to the twenty-first century,
things still collapsed into abstract, beige hills.
There were all these new details, of course:
lenses whose shutters were faster than thinking;
photos of star-sprawl; nets flecked with wavelengths
that had to be tricked into light.
Once it had seen them, however,
they all fell behind to a loose wash of brown,
the patience and grin of the slope...
As it was for each scene it encountered:
the small bones, the shopfronts, the shit;
the legs of the bipeds;
the plain where the buses came down from the hills;
the markets where birds
sang their grief very high, very fast.

Nothing resolved –
beyond unfinished tracts of rough paint –

while memory mumbled and sooked
like a litter of pups...

This is what it has learnt over two hundred years:

that details will repudiate their sigh of commonality;
that thin-fill horizons will keep rolling in;
that nothing shuts tight.

Which is why it still has
that same anxious, unsettled, eyes-everywhere look.

V

CITY

This is the city
that cast out its non-human others.
No stars but indicative twinkles.
No birds but those street-vermin – doves.

No corpses – shelves of dyed meat.

The trees stand in rows of consensus,
with caverns for bellies. The water
is managed by Furniture, Mortgage and Calm.
True, there is light – as a starting-point.
Odd times, a breeze, from offstage...

Everything else is just scripts and machines
for the narrative:
scapes of the ramp and the overpass;
glass walls of sigh
for the visual injection of need.

It is like being trapped in a tumour of signs –
motives, but no invitations.
                              Not real text,
whose others are able to speak –
                              as in poems –
but a march-past of lacks and anxieties,
where eyes have the sly look of strategies,
shrewdly deployed...

ON THE PHOTOGRAPH OF DR RANSOME WITH GERALD THE LION

This is the gloat of the sensible:
no jubilation, no elbow-and-fist –
Ransome has his arm around his guide –
and Gerald had to die for even that.
In time-honoured practice,
the trophy is placed in the foreground –
whose role is to be big enough
its hunters will grow bigger with its death.

  And Gerald? The lion looks tired –
its eyes shut, its jaw on a rock –
head propped up straight to approximate *fierce*:

who next
            will be drained of his innards
and stuffed to brand new –
then screwed to a wall of neat beasts –
also surprised to be poking their heads
through the brickwork – though all
with a modest demeanour: no scowling, no sulks...

Thence to contribute – though silent in fact –
to the radio play the good doctor conducts in his head:
with Elsa, his daughter; with Junie, his hard-drinking wife;
with guys from the Borrowdale hunt club ...
with the pricks at taxation; with Beryl, at t-ball;
his tombstone; his father; his weight –
with Smoky and Ratso, his wife's Pekinese –
a memish blancmange of submissions addressed

to the living, the dead, the invented:
in the fraught and irregular case he hopes one day to win.

THE LINE

We need to draw a line – a line of pipes –
against those who think they've a right to complain
if their tap-water smokes, or refuses to flow.
Who are these people?
And what makes them think the stuff's theirs?

And we need to draw a line – *in bright, five-storey blue* –
against those who gabble and squawk
about room for the bird with the splotchy red mush.
What is this? Coast-views for cocky?
When we're not allowed near that blade-ready, high-margin scrub?

We need to draw a line – a line of conveyor-belts –
against those who whinge about sea-levels rising –
Who bought there! Who knew how to read!
While for those who have lived there for five generations –
Ownership's no guarantee against natural events!

We need to draw a line – a line of transmission-wires –
hard, high and long: against those
who threaten the *om* of a smooth-running grid:
planting unsightly, vertiginous, sickness-inducing, bird-splattering fans
on our personal hills – our proprietary views.

And we need to draw a line:
a line of jocks – each with a weird need
to nuzzle the ears of the strong –
a line of conspiracy-theories and bog-earnest claims –
against those who *still* believe evidence:

a moist line of private anxieties;
a line of raw memories, pegged out with photos of kids;
a line of resentments, of sour gobs of hearsay;
of lost loves – the wreckage of beds –
a line of the needy, who will not – who can't afford – ever –
to weigh – or to budge.

A PERFUMED ADDRESS

My dear birds, it's true –
we weren't paying attention –
unfortunate moments ensued:
though nothing – we trust –
to detract from our kindly intent.

And I hope the sad fact
there were things we did not always grasp
has not caused you distress –
even less, led to misattributions –
like setting our ignorance down
as indifference or greed.

Because, my dear birds,
how should we know you needed old trees?

That rats came ashore with our boats?

That *your* breeds were not inexhaustible?

If, my dear riflebird,
feathers were plucked and – respectfully –
stuffed into hats:
please see that *this* was aesthetics –
no-one would go to such effort for anything less.

And if, my dear parrot,
you're sadly quite fallen away,
we hope it means something –
the shimmering, shadow-flecked blur
of your path through our sighs.

How could you argue, O songbirds,
the mist-nets you're caught with,
the wire of your homes –
your owner's tobacco-stale lips –
don't inspire your best tunes?

O birds: can't you see how we love you?
Your colours, your music, your flight...

Our taste for your kind's
a proof we are at-bottom sacred.

For who would regret more than we would
the loss of your chatter, the end of your cheek?

FALLEN ASH

Down here, weather is rumour.
As for direction: who knows?
There are only the tall and the fallen:
is that not enough? Once,
weather swirled through my branches.
Falling, I trailed cloud and glare.
Now, sky's knit back into leaf-net –
sunbeams, their eddying motes...
It will take longer to slump, to relax
into soil. Not that before I fell earthwards
I wasn't, already, a city of frass:
ant-crumble; trunk-buttressed mulch ...
My hollows will knit with fine rigging.
I shall turn into nest-wall,
be reconstituted as pulp.
I shall trail atoms, air by calm air.
My xylem will swell with the fibres of fungi.
Nights, I shall glow with their fruit.
Blue wrens will sing me as boundary;
devils sleep curled in my caves.
Orchids will rest on me,
saplings drive through me for sky...
I shall grow derelict, mangy with emerald,
sink beneath leaves' lightest rains –
add the damp silence of loam
to the silence of shadow.

WIND

Lying awake, while the southerly
drives at the forest:
slows to a rumble,
then pauses, and wails somewhere else –
each new attack
a pitched scream at untested terrain...

Seeing each note as a colour –
disjointed modernist humours
of banshee and brain...

But trees will go down,
and shed walls go down;
the nest of the robin
explode into dendrites and fluff.
This is the earth
that has still never spoken our name.
Tonight, it will play with its offspring:
scatter their promenades,
smash through the airs
of integrity, aesthetics, style –
peel back our stories
and shred them to waifs of transition ...

Nights like tonight,
you could mumble thin reason –
but find only waves of thick air
that know nothing of plans.

MAGPIES

Bright-eyed and stary –

with heads cocked
at all the wrong angles –

like poets:

astonished –
bewildered –
by all the wrong things.

CAT'S CLAW

Glittering and ecstatic,
they skite in the afternoon sun –
holding their arms out to scare us –
splay-scribble monsters of vine:
each with its dead one –
        its silky-oak mummy –
                its river-oak guy –
        in its leaf-cavern guts ...

A circus-troupe call for assassins –
punks in mock-tragical attitudes
        hazing the creek –
so proud of themselves
and their smother
of suck, shade and scrawl –
their benzedrine air-show of tendrils –

proud, above all, of the way
that they hustled the sun-gift
        with three unco nets –
from big shots
of free-standing lignin:
these *bones with their shawls.*

Cat's Claw: an invasive creeper; these at Amamoor, SE Queensland.

WATTLE

The wattle
is losing the plot.

What once
was a modest emission
of filigreed pewter and ungainly sticks
is all leaven-and-bloat:
engorged to a pale-yellow nebula –
caverns of bract.
Soon, when I look out my door,
there will be no sky left:
just a field of bright minor –
a mattress of luminous puffs.
Those things I rant about:
'poems and their ear for the other',
'the bodily proof' –
will be muffled by whorls –
while memory's sleights
clutch at lemon
in which all pasts drown...
nothing remain except glare:
the nodding and heave
of meticulous, pre-timed explosions;
knucklets and baseball gloves
loaded with star-wheels, coronas –
all set for the show...

At which, the most restive clusters
will ionise, glow...

IRONBARK

An ironbark –
in a paddock of blonde tufts and stone.

Not 'regular curves
of an optimum access to water' –
but taut, stubborn choices
for line and its elbows,
a charcoal with scratches and lumps.

No 'bounty of nourishment: symmetry,
unhampered growth' –
but: root-cells like rust –
a mitotic insistence...

from whose leaves –
those loose mists of blades –
one could hardly seek shade.

Like a poem of hard truths,
whose one gift is its presence...

EASY

How easy on the eye
the weight of clouds:
their change of state
collapsing into light.

How dreamy the ocean:
its pulses and spills;
its slow churn of rock;
its indifference.

And how like a place
we were built to inhabit,
this earth, with its green veins, its air;
its shelving and luminous prospects...

COASTING

The lantern-fish gulp through the press of lamp black,
the chloroplasts dance in the sun,
while Mrs Petunia buys spots for her teapots,
at one thousand k's every breath.

The cranes duck and rear, and twine necks in the snow,
the sunspots and algal blooms flare,
while Kylie-Ann scrolls through the bidets and basins,
at one thousand k's every breath.

The pink lagoon fills with the sans-serif inkblots of waders,
the shearwaters skim through the gale,
while Dunstan imbibes his Prime Minister's keywords,
at one thousand k's every breath.

The blue wrens dot-strobe through the thicket,
the fumaroles luminesce green,
while eloquent poets review their Selecteds,
at one thousand k's every breath.

WATER

As long as there is water,
I belong:

Tides underfoot in the boathouse –
the pulsing of ripples –
sine-waves of dream between boards.

      Faint rings of rain
      on a bright glass
            of tumbledown sandstone
      and upside-down trees.

   Lichens – grey droplets of time –
   at work on broken-backed rocks
   where the earth shrinks and swells...

I, too, a shape-shifter,
morphing through passions and tales:

a loosely-bagged stream
in an intimate race with its shadows.

      Without it,
      there's only a skit
      for explosions and impacts;

      a pie-farce for numbers, not words;

a Gothic late, late show
where none of the cast bids us welcome
and nobody laughs.

THE TERN

It has ploughed with its throat
through the sandbar,
fluffed itself up and pushed down
with each side of its nape.
It can't wait for feathers to settle,
but hollows its shoulders
and shudders its beak –
like a drill –
through each side of its breast.

It holds up its wings
like a bruiser –
as if it might scare them away.

Then it vibrates its tail.

But the lice will not go.

No jabbing, no shaking will do.

The other birds stare at horizons –
or half close their eyes on one leg –

hunch and drift off
while it spasms and preens for its life.

The big rolling surf, its bright levels,
the gulls with their just-in-time flights:
everything here's as it should be
on loud, vivid earth –

apart from the ghost
with the crumpled straw hat
watching, appalled, from the beach.

PLAINS

Wherever you look from's
a flat, subtle rise –
sightlines unbroken
in every low-shrubbed non-direction.
Unlike protuberant lands –
where answer or end
is around the next corner, or hill –
here, it's down every long vector:
a stage-set with nothing but clouds,
and then sky, and then clouds –
where distance from purpose
is measured in hours to horizons
you never get near –
in patient, provisional journeys
down panels of sky-blue,
and royal blue,
and pale and improbable aqua.

THE GULLS

They slide over ripples and gleams
   in pursuit of half-glimpses, low
over ankle-deep water, with stiff,
   screwed-down necks: dyspeptic uncles
who stare with whom no-one agrees.
   They harry the gull with the fish
then the gull with the fish.
   Strutting through kelp they can see
there's no point but they still
   bleat and scratch pick and shrug.
If, on occasion, they tilt west and circle
   ghost-calling cat-calling
medleys of spleen and desire, it's not
   that they do not despair
of their vagueness of speech.
   They are sick of the sea its horizons
its grey its indifference its jokes.
   They are sick of the poor spread
of wet chips and misshapen lumps.
   Beaks clamped on not giving in,
they drift to the shore to consider
   to scrunch down and wait:
querulous prayers who know
   only too well sea outlasts them;
who also know without desire
   no bird escapes the patience of the sea.

VI

MINIMS

Not so different, in intent,
from the suave semiotics
of suits at the Club –
survivors from metal bands
trumping each other
with tales of heroic indulgence:
Tuesdays to Saturdays,
Mondays from two, at half-price.

~

Messiaen's new modernist God:
where the swell's invocation's
   replaced
by the *presence*
of winds and percussion.

~

The open voice
lives in a pure world:
abstracted from all
but emotion.

Tighten it –
close the throat down –
and it tilts towards speech –

and the roughhouse
of *différance*.

~

AFTER THE CIVIL WAR

One of the kinder blooms:

that the cornets and reeds
of the marches that primed troops to die
should have grown playful pauses
        and half steps –
and shuffled and chiacked their way
up the main street as jazz.

~

WRITING STALIN

No point
in hurling the small stones
of underweight rebels:

as Dmitri found out –

who could only
write the nightmare
once he knew
what it was to be broken.

~

Tough for the faith of the chorus –
the modernist's robust
but playful experiments...

~

THE MEISTERSINGER

A fantasy
of reward for true art.

But it feels a little Disney:
as if the moral
were the motive of the tale –
ending so sure, so rewarding,
that only a child –
or an artist with needs –
could subscribe.

~

The American dream
and the blues
    are conjoined:
each is an expression
    of the other.

~

NICO, CHRISSIE AMPHLETT, MARIANNE FAITHFULL:

Who'd refused
to insist on their looks –

but were angry and hurt,
like the girl
who'd thought beauty would save her.

~

To the pure rock fan,
justice and kindness are wet:

if you've come
for the hormones of status –
what use is this *should*?

~

Nobody knew, at the time,
but the allies pushed on, through the mud,
for the right of the Beatles
to dress up in *very* bright uniforms.

~

If, like Mahler,
your key trope's arrival:
you'll soon find yourself
at the rear of a shape-shifting mist
with the griefs of farewell.

~

Carols and shanties,
anthems and hymns:
sung by the spot-lit,
they tonsil, embroider and trill –
music whose point is *together* –
to be one of many –
find more strength as one...

~

CIVIL RIGHTS

The first claim
was for the right to exist:
all they could do
was announce they were there –
Armstrong and Ellington:
ballsy, but wary, polite.

Next came equality:
no other option
for Dizzy or Monk
but to blow up
that careful, wrought beauty...

~

An undertow, in English music –
in Vaughan-Williams' Tallis,
the Purcell pavanes –
the tug of alternative currents –
a lack of belief in the surface,
the ground-rules of form...

~

No problem,
in jazz,
with the ending:
not having laid down a statement
the piece must resolve.

~

Miles at the Vanguard –
Monk at the Blue Note:

a few dozen hands
and their echoes
clap *gigs for all time.*

~

Music tries to speak
and language tries to sing

and meaning
tugs at both
with the beak of a vulture.

~

Selfies –
the hunt for more friends –

if you lean
with your ear to the net,
you can hear Janet Baker
descending –
one note at a time –
down the spirals
of Dido's lament.[1]

---

1. I.e., singing: "Remember me, remember me..." (Cf 'When I am laid in earth', Henry
   Purcell, *Dido and Aeneas*, Decca 423 720-2, 1961/1990)

~

NICK DRAKE:

Who found a music
for the nakedness of *naked*.

~

Country refuses abandon:

in its world, you never know
what you'll be dealing with next.

~

To take a show tune
and transpose it into jazz –

to give it a blue note,
and teach it to swing –

was to enter a war:

one involving
heroin, and attitude –
grenades of proprietary slang –

was to picket a permanent line
between *keeping things steady*
and *letting things rip* –

in a stand-off beyond resolution.

~

SHOSTAKOVICH:

For whom
the brassy works
were preparation
for the gutted ones.

~

Blues is not display.

The heroes could not play it
as a vehicle for heroes.

Not till they'd removed themselves.

(Though even then
the people came for heroes).

~

THE SOLOISTS

The cats wait –
in turn –
for their blow:

because the ego –
and its precedents –
are strict
as any score.

~

LISZT:

Teases, delays, false directions:

that the master of *cunning ways home*
should have so lost his way...

~

In Dvorak,
both the US
and Bohemia
sound the same.

One can see
how American spaces
can beckon the phrase
to be airier – more optimistic:

but what tuned Bohemian ears
to such mild prairie dawns?

~

Without the naïveté of the sixties –

who did not know
what they could not think –

there'd be none of the difficult truths
that the fifties refused.

~

BONNIE RAITT

A voice
which refuses
the permanent loss:

which has shifted love's pain
to the back of the throat –

which has traded emotional range
for the virtue of strength.

~

Resonant bumps
and stage whispers –
the chord of an aria
waiting for business to cease:

a version of home
on a planet
where all homes dissolve...

~

The open voice
looks for a chair
when the drummer tunes up:

you can't listen *and* dance.

~

Would the Beethoven Six
invoke sand-dunes
if that were the scene
we had learnt for such cues?

~

OPERA (ACT V):

Consciousness
on planet earth:

those sostenutos
of realization...

~

THE VIOLIN (SARASATE, CHAUSSON etc)

Once its mere use
was a proof of sincerity,
no-one believed anymore.

~

No longer willing
to extrapolate,
five minutes of song
is as much
as we feel we can offer.

~

Buried, in a warehouse,
in Vienna, or Berlin –
all the business of transcendence,
neatly stacked:
timpani – and Wagner tubas;
a schedule of fees for more strings;
an angel's repair-kit –
gold stage boxes, steps –
in an unscripted peace of arrival.

~

Over and over,
we crank the significance pedals:
tutti and dominants –
drums, and orgasmatron blues...

And over and over,
significance fades
like the clearest of unblemished skies.

~

The voice
insists on centre-stage:

painful,
if instruments
shoulder it off to the edges.

What hope have we got?

~

How best to engage
with the high pitch of Strauss
when it's humid, and thirty degrees?

~

The husband looks baffled again:
how, without a sense of what is missing,
will he register the loss the piece invokes?

~

BARBER, DELIUS, HOLST:

Those images
of a non-triumphal paradise:
each generation re-invents them.

While the always-credible tropes
of desire and esteem
just march onwards, unchallenged.

~

In music,
as in poetry,
subjunctive's the resonant tense:

playing the wound
between how things are,
how they might be...

~

Year after year:
the cohorts of hormones
in sync through the Spotify lists
with their once-only tastes.

~

No joy
in Hank Williams –
only the unsmiling chords
of the prison of love.

~

IN THE NORTH

Some climates teach you:

to wait for the earth to unfreeze;
for the one, precious crop to grow tall;

that heaven is distant –
that home keys *must be* far away.

~

Impossible to specify arrival
or articulate its joys.

So music
which desires such things
becomes a meditation on the portent.

VII

SEA CLIFF

A cavern of wave-slump
and suction so casual
you search
for each half-glimpse of plastic
that once had a point.

Slick water streaming
        like blood
through a carnivore's teeth.

Nowhere to start from
and nowhere to end
where the waves thud and hiss –
and the one thing they say
is *More flotsam, more chaos, more wrack.*

Sheer rock fades back –
        but you still see enough
to know every small link in your alibi –
each temperate claim –
        will be mush in these claws:

nightmare that rears without trying...

Like a dictator's cutie in folk-dress,
you could walk through the Gross Fugue –
or hold out a tray full of poems.

But no smear of virtuous twinkling
        will pacify this.

Last birds call out for their hollows.

Soon, you'll head back
to your warm box of rough calculations –
shut your eyes tight, and stare down:
at gleams of insouciant masses, lurching
and dropping beneath you, and slapping, all night.

Notes

"The Mooncalves": "so you too, praise Culloden" – Handel wrote *Judas Maccabaeus* to celebrate the Duke of Cumberland's victory at Culloden; "Nadehzda and Osip" – in 1938, the Mandelstams had been living in internal exile at Voronezh, when the news came through – as they had feared – that Osip would have to leave for Siberia.

"The Brisbane Longeurs": i.e., Peter Porter, Kevin Hart, David Malouf and Rhyll McMaster.

"Charmian": Together with the works of Clift and George Johnston, this poem owes a debt to Nadia Wheatley's wonderful biography, *The Life and Myth of Charmian Clift* (Harper/Collins, 2001).

"Goya's Dog": c.f. "El Perro", c. 1820, Museo del Prado, Madrid.

"The Line": "the bird with the splotchy red mush" is the swift parrot, a sometime visitor to the bush in Sydney's northern peninsula, where this poem was first presented.

"Coasting": "One thousand k's every breath" is the (very) approximate speed of the Milky Way relative to the other galaxies in its local cluster.

Minims: "Writing Stalin" – Dmitri is Dmitri Shostakovich.

Acknowledgements

"Fallen Ash" appeared in Spanish in *Aji Arbolarium: Antologia Poetica de los Cinco Continents* ed. Marcela Yukuna, a joint publication of Colegio José Max Léon (Colombia), and Editorial Echarpen (Argentina), in 2018; and in English, in *on first looking*, ed. J. Kent, D. Musgrave and C. Ricketts, Puncher and Wattmann, 2018. "The Boy from the War Veterans' Home" was published in *Measures of Truth, the Newcastle Poetry Prize Anthology*, ed. J. Beveridge and M. Ladd, 2020. An earlier version of "Airport" appeared in The Wonderbook, ed. Kit Kelen (Macao University Writing School, 2015), and this version in the Australian Poetry Anthology, volume 9, 2021. "The Line" was published in "The Spirit of the Collection", ed. L. Wicks, Meuse Press, 2016.

Lightning Source UK Ltd.
Milton Keynes UK
UKHW042211150822
407319UK00014B/918